The Children We Remember

by

CHANA BYERS ABELLS

Photographs from the Archives
of Yad Vashem, The Holocaust Martyrs'
and Heroes' Remembrance Authority
Jerusalem, Israel

 Greenwillow Books, New York

ACKNOWLEDGEMENTS

To my husband, Zvi, for his help;

To photographer Zvi Reiter for his cooperation;

To Dr. Shmuel Krakowski, Director of Archives at Yad Vashem,
who gave me the opportunity to learn about my people's heroism
and martyrdom; and

To my children, Sharona, Gila, and Deena, who, but for time
and space, might have shared the fate of *The Children We
Remember.*
C. B. A.

First published in 1983 by Kar-Ben Copies, Inc.
Redesigned in 1986 by Greenwillow Books.
Copyright © 1983, 1986 by Chana Byers Abells
All rights reserved. No part of this
book may be reproduced or utilized in
any form or by any means, electronic or
mechanical, including photocopying,
recording or by any information storage
and retrieval system, without permission
in writing from the Publisher,
Greenwillow Books, a division
of William Morrow & Company, Inc.,
105 Madison Avenue, New York, N.Y. 10016.
Printed in Hong Kong by South China Printing Co.
First Edition
10 9 8 7 6 5 4 3 2 1

Library of Congress
Cataloging-in-Publication Data
Abells, Chana Byers.
The children we remember.
Summary: Text and photographs briefly describe
the fate of Jewish children after the Nazis
began to control their lives.
   1. Holocaust, Jewish (1939-1945)—Pictorial
works—Juvenile literature.   2. Jewish
children—Pictorial works—Juvenile literature.
[1. Holocaust, Jewish (1939-1945)]
I. Yad va-shem, rashut ha-zikaron
la-Sho'ah vela-gevurah.   II. Title.
D810.J4A23   1986   940.53'161   85-24876
ISBN 0-688-06371-3
ISBN 0-688-06372-1 (lib. bdg.)

This book is dedicated to
the children whose lives ended
during the Holocaust and to the
photographers, known and unknown,
who risked their lives
to record their story.

Before the Nazis...

Some children lived in towns like this,

went to schools like this,

prayed in synagogues like this,

played with their friends,

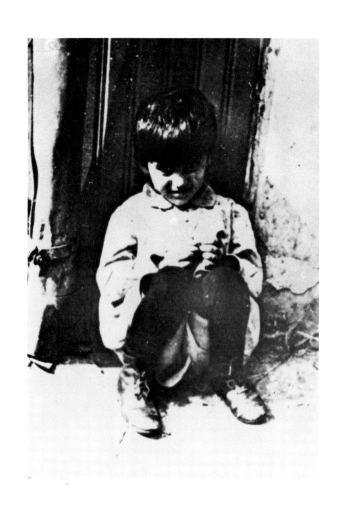

or sat alone.

Then the Nazis came.

They made the Jews
sew patches
on their clothes.

They closed Jewish stores and schools.

They burned synagogues.

They took away homes,

and families were forced to live in the streets.

When the children were cold,

they wrapped themselves in rags.

When the children were hungry,

they shared the little food they had.

The children helped the old, the sick,

and each other.

The Nazis hated the children
because they were Jews.

Sometimes they took them away
from their families
and sent them far from home.

Sometimes

they put children to death.

These children were killed by the Nazis:

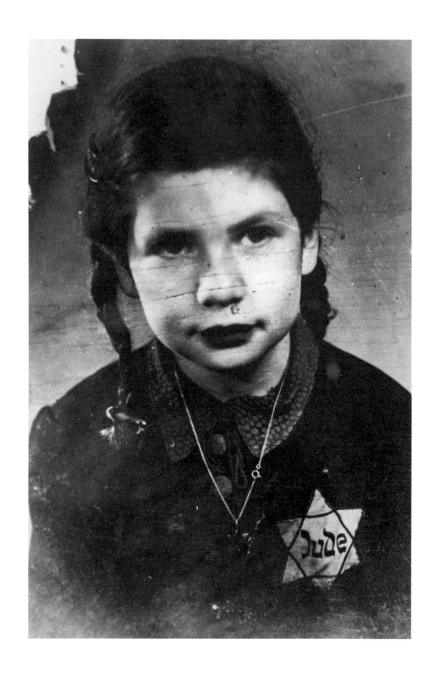

Chana

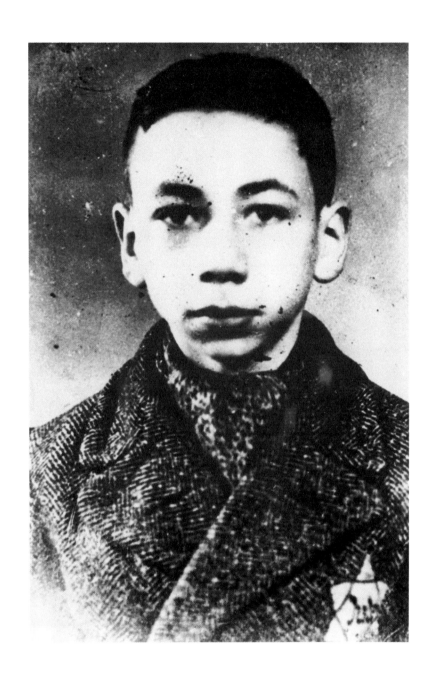

her brother

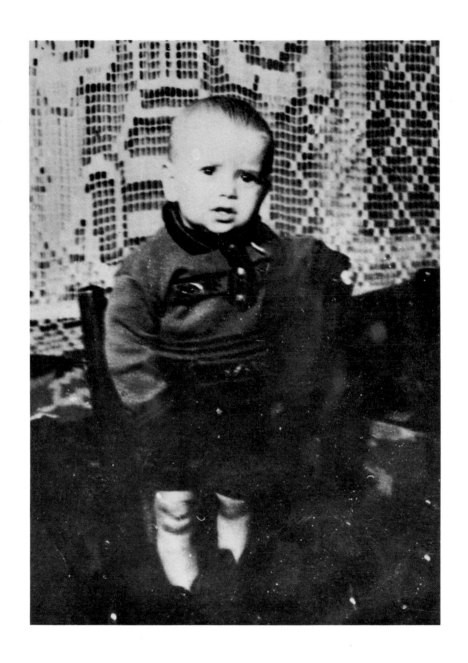

Willie

and children whose names
we do not know.

But some children survived.

Some escaped to Israel and other countries.

Some were rescued by Christian families.

Others hid in forests

or pretended to be non-Jews.

The children who survived are grown now.

Some have children of their own.

They live in towns like yours,

go to schools like yours,

play with their friends, or sit alone…

Just like the children we remember.